DARE TO LOVE AGAIN

Poems of Resilience, Hope, and Second Chance Romance

Taylor Quill

I

TABLE OF CONTENTS

CHAPTER ONE

Shattered Hearts

Bitter Remedy

I taste the bitter bite of memory,
Like spoiled wine poured cold into my veins.
Each drop a cruel, clinging remedy,
It burns, then freezes, rusted into chains.

The echo of your voice in crowded rooms,
A hollow hum that haunts me everywhere.
It lingers in the night, in darkened tombs,
And cuts the air with pain I can't repair.

Glass Hearts

I see your shadow dance behind closed eyes,
In broken glass, where fallen dreams reside.
Your voice, a lull, a whispered lullaby,
Now cold and sharp, a blade where love once
lied.

I feel the crack, the break, the quiet snap,
That silent shatter no one hears but me.
A fragile heart, a crystal in a trap,
Now dust and fragments scattered carelessly.

And yet, your taste, like sugar turned to stone,
Remains upon my tongue, though all is gone.

Salt and Silence

Salt upon my tongue, I feel it,
Bitter proof of tears unhealed.
Hollow echoes, empty spaces,
Words unsaid, and broken traces.
In the silence, something shatters,
All our love reduced to tatters.

Echoes in the Dark

I hear you in the hollow dark,
Your voice, a ghost I can't erase.
A fading spark, a hidden mark.

Each room we shared, now cold and stark,
Memories lost without a trace.
I hear you in the hollow dark.

What once was warm now leaves me stark,
As silence fills the empty space—
A fading spark, a hidden mark.

No longer here to light my arc,
Love's bitter echo gone to waste.
I hear you in the hollow dark,
A fading spark, a hidden mark

Ashes on the Tongue

A taste of ashes lingers, dry and deep,
the residue of words we left unsaid.
Each sound, a splinter, sharp against my tongue,
like shards of glass left scattered in the dark.

I feel the heavy weight of emptiness,
the hollow press of all that love once held—
warm whispers, softened sighs,
now cold, and cut like fractured dreams,
their echoes ringing in an empty room.

CHAPTER TWO

Echoes of What Was

Bittersweet

I taste the tang of old goodbyes,
Like wine that's soured with the years.
A sip recalls your whispered lies,
Each drop reborn as salted tears.

The sweetness gone, the glass half-full,
Yet lips still ache to drink it down.
The memory's sharp, the nights are dull,
And past's last sip a lover's frown.

Silken Silence

I feel the ghostly trace your hands once drew,
Soft silken warmth, a velvet touch I knew.
The sheets still bear the shadowed shape of you,
In silent folds where old desires grew.

The weight of love, like whispers caught in thread,
Now wraps around this hollow, empty bed.

The Echo of Your Laughter

Your laughter, it lingers and rings,
A memory feathered with wings.
I hear it at night,
Though lost from my sight,
A song that the emptiness sings.

Each note that you left haunts the room,
A melody stitched to my gloom.
It dances and fades,
In lilting cascades,
Yet lingers like old perfume.

Fragrance of Forever

The scent of you—cinnamon, spice, and pine,
Drifts through these halls like a haunting song.
Where you once stood, memories throng,
A fragrance trapped in ghostly vine.

It wraps me close, a silent sigh,
A whispered trace that won't comply.

Through a Window of Rain

I watch you again
through the fogged glass of my mind,
in muted gray and silver tones—
the rain paints our past, blurred and bent,
each drop a time I could not forget.

You are there, smiling
like some ghost in winter,
half-formed and forever out of reach.
I can almost feel your touch
through the glass, cool against my fingertips,
as I press and wait,
but you dissolve into the rain—
no more than mist,
an echo I can only see.

CHAPTER THREE

Doubts and Defenses

Bitter Tastes

I taste the salt of what you left,
A bitter bite of love's deceit.
My guarded heart, a fortress kept,
Where broken promises retreat.

The flavor clings, it lingers long,
In every word, I hide the past.
I fear your lips would prove me wrong,
Yet walls I've built hold steadfast, fast.

The Fortress

I built these walls so high,
Bricks bold and black and cold.
Each lie another stone stacked by,
To guard what once was bold.

Inside, the silence hums,
A hollow, empty drum.
Yet outside where your footsteps come,
I freeze, refuse to run.

Echoes I Can't Unhear

In the quiet corners of night,
whispers waft like wind, wary and worn.
I hear the hollow sounds of promises past,
echoes etched in everything you touched.

Walls that once felt warm now wail,
crumbling, cracked in cold distrust,
and every sound seems sharper here—
the scrape of sorrow,
the rasp of regret,
the distant drip of faith dissolved.

Blind to Light

I shut my eyes to love's once-blinding light,
preferring shadows cast from doubt and fear.
For trust's sweet taste has soured in the night,
its echoes sharp, too heavy now to bear.

I clench the strings that tether close my heart,
a threadbare knot grown tighter with each tear.
Too soft to break, too fragile to restart,
too rough to dare let someone linger there.

And so I hide from what I cannot see,
where love once lit, distrust has dimmed the way.
If I can't feel the truth, let lies be free;
it's safer here, where memories decay.

Yet still a voice within me hums and sings—
a whisper soft of softer, kinder things.

Scent of Smoke

The scent of smoke still haunts the air I breathe,
remains of trust gone up in flame and ash.
Each spark a scar that hides what lies beneath.
I tried to pull in breath, though lungs would seethe,
from charred remains of what we could not last.
The scent of smoke still haunts the air I breathe.

It's burnt in bone, the dust I can't unsheathe,
a taste of loss too sharp, the memory rash.
Each spark a scar that hides what lies beneath.

Yet in the ashes, seeds of something seethe,
a chance to breathe without the past's rehash.
The scent of smoke still haunts the air I breathe,

and every flame is tamed to soothe and sheath
the scars, the shadows that my heart enmash.
Each spark a scar that hides what lies beneath—

if love is fire, then let its heat belie
the scent of smoke still haunts the air I breathe.

CHAPTER FOUR

Healing in the Ruins

Bittersweet Balm

In silent rooms where shadows softly sweep,
The taste of healing bitter but so deep.
I close my eyes and feel the wounds unwind,
The scars grow lighter, softer in my mind.

I hear the whispered notes of old refrains,
Their echoes thinning, lost in softer pains.
Each memory's edge, once sharp as shards of glass,
Now dulled by time, begins to dim and pass.

The fragrance of forgiveness fills the air,
A balm to soothe the places torn and bare.
I see, at last, the ruins turn to grace,
New growth now finds its roots within this space.

And in the taste of all that I've released,
I find, at last, a soft and quiet peace.

Lingering Notes

I walk the silent streets at dawn,
The sky, a soft and silver gray,
And hear the night's last whisper gone,
Its echoes fading fast away.

Each breath tastes sweet, yet bitter still,
As if the past yet clings to me.
But with each step, I feel the thrill—
Of learning how to simply be.

Dust Settles Slowly

Dust settles, softly seen, silver in morning light,
Coating the corners I never thought to clear.
I taste time's gentle grit on my tongue,
Feel it cling like memory,
Fine and faint, yet present, persistent.

There is forgiveness in the air, faint and full,
Faint like the first time you let pain go,
Feeling, not fleeing—finding peace
Where jagged edges once held reign.

Now, I am learning to be still,
To breathe without wincing,
To let the quiet settle,
Smoothing the roughness within.

A Sip of Silence

I sip the silence, cool and slow,
A taste of calm in every breath,
The feel of peace I barely know,
Healing the spaces left by death.

A taste of calm in every breath,
A quiet clearing in my mind,
Healing the spaces left by death,
Where shadows soften, less defined.

A quiet clearing in my mind,
Forgiveness floats like fallen leaves.
Where shadows soften, less defined,
My heart releases, aches relieved.

Forgiveness floats like fallen leaves,
The feel of peace I barely know.
My heart releases, aches relieved—
I sip the silence, cool and slow.

Piece by Piece

Piece by piece, I find my way,
Where broken bits once lay in dust,
To mend the wounds of yesterday.

Each fragment, sharp, was left to stay,
To taunt with tales of lost-born trust—
Piece by piece, I find my way.

I feel the edges smooth, give sway,
The jagged pain turns slow to rust,
I mend the wounds of yesterday.

I taste the warmth of dawn's new day,
Forgive the fractures born of lust—
Piece by piece, I find my way.

Where echoes once held tight as prey,
Now silence settles, soft and just—
To mend the wounds of yesterday,
Piece by piece, I find my way.

CHAPTER FIVE

Learning to Stand Alone

Taste of Freedom

To taste the tang of freedom on my tongue,
Where once my love and bitter fears had clung.
The spice of solitude, so strange and bright,
A taste that deepens slowly in the night.

I feast on hours my own, no need to share,
No hands to hold, no promises to tear.
My own soft breath, a comfort sweet and new,
A rich and rare, resilient rendezvous.

The days unfurl like petals on a vine,
And every sip of silence feels like wine.
To learn, to know, my heart belongs to me—
In tasting this, I learn to just *be free*.

The Feel of My Own Skin

My skin's my shelter, strong and soft,
A cloak I wear with pride.
I feel the pulse of heart aloft,
No need for you beside.

My hands are warm with strength alone,
I carry what I find.
This journey's mine, my seeds are sown,
With roots that calmly bind.

The feel of earth beneath my feet,
Reminds me I am whole.
I hold myself, my own heartbeat,
A balm to fill my soul.

The Echo of Quiet

Echoes fill the room,
gentle beats of silence fall—
I learn to hear *me*.

No more voices flood,
no more calls to break my peace,
just soft space to breathe.

Alone, I find strength,
a sound that steadies the night,
the echo of *me*.

What I See in Myself

I see in myself a spark that grows bright,
No shadows from past loves can darken this flame.
I stand on my own, alone in the light.

The world fades away in deep, starry night,
Yet I'm rooted firm, secure in my name.
I see in myself a spark that grows bright.

Once lost in his shadow, hidden from sight,
But I found in this solitude no shame—
I stand on my own, alone in the light.

With each rising sun, a bold new delight,
The vision of who I am, free of blame.
I see in myself a spark that grows bright.

This journey is mine; I welcome its height,
Uncovering parts of me, shedding old blame—
I stand on my own, alone in the light.

Each day brings a joy, unmeasured by fright,

In mirrors, I find a face that's reclaimed.

I see in myself a spark that grows bright,

I stand on my own, alone in the light.

The Taste, the Feel of Me

I savor my own laughter, crisp and true,

Its taste an orchard ripe with fruit,

and with each sweet bite,

I find myself anew.

I feel the silk of my own skin,

the brush of fingertips gentle,

a touch I once longed for in others,

but found, finally,

was softest from myself.

I hear my own song, unsung for years,

a rhythm pulsing, a steady beat.

The noise of others faded,

leaving only the sound of me—

bold, warm, and loud enough to fill the room.

I see in shadows on walls,

the figure of a soul at peace,

and in this sight, this sense, this taste of me,

I learn to stand,

perfectly alone, and free.

CHAPTER SIX

Rediscovering Hope

Whispers of Dawn

I taste the morning's sweet and silent grace,
As light breaks through, a golden whisper spread,
A warmth that fills the empty, aching space,
Reviving dreams I thought were long since dead.

I feel the gentle breath of hope arise,
Soft sunlight soothing shadows sharp and cold;
It blooms beneath the open, waking skies,
A timid touch that starts to take its hold.

I hear the song of life in new refrain,
A melody in every simple sound,
A hymn that hums in harmony with pain,
Yet lifts the heart from sorrow's solid ground.

I see the world anew in morning's hue,
And dare to dream that love could dawn anew.

A Taste of Tomorrow

A taste of tomorrow, like fresh summer rain,
Sweet as it trickles, dissolving the pain.
Soft, subtle flavors—so gentle, so pure—
A sip of belief that love might endure.

Feel the faint pulse of hope's quiet beat,
Growing with grace as it gathers its heat.
The warmth on my skin, a soft, steady hum,
Hinting that something sweet is to come.

Senses Awaken

I hear the world's soft promise in the breeze,
A lullaby that love could yet return,
As tender whispers drift from silent trees.

I feel the rush of warmth, the gentle ease,
In every shaded grove and sunlit turn,
I hear the world's soft promise in the breeze.

The subtle taste of peace, as fresh as seas,
Within my soul, it starts to hum and burn,
As tender whispers drift from silent trees.

I see a path ahead that leads to peace,
A road where light and shadows twist and churn;
I hear the world's soft promise in the breeze.

And though the past can press, it finds release—
A hope begins, too bright to yet discern,
As tender whispers drift from silent trees.

A heart can heal in time, with gentle ease;
I hear the world's soft promise in the breeze,
As tender whispers drift from silent trees.

First Bloom

Morning's bright breath wakes,
dancing on the skin like spring—
a promise of bloom.

I taste dawn's first blush,
soft as berries, sweet and sure,
a hint of the light.

A petal, trembling,
feels like hope's soft, tender pulse,
steady as heartbeats.

New leaves sprout and stretch,
reaching for light, love, and air—
I begin to trust.

Light's Return

I feel the light, a flame that softly grows,
The smallest flicker glowing in the dark,
Its warmth unfurls, a seedling's green repose,
A fragile pulse, yet sharp enough to spark.

I taste the air, as sweet as meadow's lark,
The tender notes, as life begins to hum—
And from the shadows, silent hopes become.

CHAPTER SEVEN

Letting Go and Moving On

Bitter to Sweet

I tasted bitter words you spoke,
A mouthful of regret,
But time dissolved each jagged note,
And healed what I'd forget.

Now honey coats the salted past,
The hurt fades, faint and slow.
Each memory is left uncast—
A candle's final glow.

The Last Echo

Your voice, a faint and distant song,
I hear its notes but not its ache.
The echo fades—it won't be long.

Once loud and sharp, it now feels wrong,
A shadowed past I must forsake.
Your voice, a faint and distant song.

The chords I used to cling upon
Grow soft as morning starts to break;
The echo fades—it won't be long.

I'll walk alone where I belong,
Unburdened by the years I wake.
Your voice, a faint and distant song.

Now harmony is mine to sing,
No longer tied to old heartbreak.
The echo fades—it won't be long.

Ashes of You

I feel the cool breeze,
a soft hush over still waves—
your heat's drifted on.

Bitter taste of smoke
lingers, a taste now fading,
ashes swept away.

Colors shifting hues,
your shadow gone from my sight,
a breath of silence.

Sight of a New Dawn

The sight of dawn now greets me fresh and true,
Its golden light unbinds my grieving heart.
The world in morning's blush is bright and new,
And here I find the strength to stand apart.

I feel the softness of the earth below,
The grass beneath my steps, a welcome guide.
No more do whispered words weigh down my soul,
No bitterness left waiting to confide.

I taste the sweetness of my own delight,
The freedom found in life's renewing hand.
With every step, I shed the hollow night,
And hold to dreams like footprints in the sand.

For now, your memory fades into the sea—
A past released, where I am finally free.

The Last Thread

I feel the pull of one last thread,
frayed and faded, thin and torn,
a tethered string, no longer worn
around my pulse, my veins, my stead.

Your voice was a taste like rust on tongue,
a sharp metallic ache, thick and sour—
but now it drips away like rain,
a dullness drained by autumn's hour.

I see the sky shift from gray to blue,
hear quiet rustling leaves in flight.
Your shadow slips, a shade anew—
I step forward, into the light.

CHAPTER EIGHT

Choosing Vulnerability

Whispers of Courage

In the quiet corners of my heart,
Whispers of courage softly start.
Like raindrops dancing on thirsty ground,
Can I trust the love that's yet to be found?

Fingers trembling, I touch the air,
A fluttering hope in a silent prayer.
The taste of sweetness, a risk so real,
To love again, to truly feel.

A Fragile Dance

With every heartbeat, I take a chance,
In this fragile dance, I must advance.
Tread lightly on dreams, let the rhythm flow,
But fears entwine like vines that grow.

The taste of fear, bittersweet on my tongue,
Yet echoes of laughter still softly hum.
Will the music of love drown the doubt,
In the embrace of trust, can I twist and shout?

The Edge of Trust

I stand at the edge, the abyss below,
Glimmers of love, can I dare to go?
The pulse of the night, like thunder, it calls,
Will I leap into light, or fear my fall?

I see the stars twinkling in skies so wide,
Yet shadows of doubt loom on every side.
The sound of your voice, a sweet serenade,
But what if it fades, and I'm left dismayed?

Fingers of Fear

Fingers of fear claw at my chest,
Yet the warmth of your gaze feels like a quest.
In the depths of despair, a flicker ignites,
A spark of connection in long, lonely nights.

The taste of your laughter, like honeyed delight,
Can I savor this moment, embrace the light?
With each step I take, my heart starts to mend,
In the dance of our souls, can I trust and pretend?

Beneath the Surface

Beneath the surface, where shadows reside,
I wrestle with doubt and the tears that I hide.
Yet the scent of your presence, like blossoms in spring
Prompts me to ponder the joy love can bring.

The sound of your heartbeat a rhythmic refrain,
Pulls me from solitude, embraces the pain.
With a taste of your kindness, so tender, so true,
Can I learn to believe, to dare to love you?

CHAPTER NINE

Love Renewed

Taste of Connection

In twilight's glow, our laughter spills,
Sweet as summer, the air it thrills.
Your voice, a whisper, soft and light,
Like honeyed tea on a cozy night.

Our fingers intertwine, a gentle dance,
With every glance, I find romance.
The taste of your kiss, a tender delight,
Unfurling petals in the warmth of night.

The Feel of You

In every heartbeat, a new refrain,
Soft as silk, our love remains.
I trace the lines of your embrace,
A woven tapestry, a sacred space.

With breaths that mingle, we rise and fall,
Wrapped in warmth, we have it all.
The feel of your skin, a soothing balm,
In your arms, I find my calm.

Echoes of Laughter

Through sunlit days and starlit skies,
Your laughter dances, a sweet surprise.
Each note, a melody that fills the air,
A symphony of joy, a love so rare.

With every word, you draw me near,
In this connection, there's nothing to fear.
The echoes of laughter, bright and clear,
Create a chorus I long to hear.

Vision of Us

I see us painting dreams anew,
Colors brighter in the morning dew.
Your eyes, twin stars that shine so bright,
Guiding my heart through the velvet night.

With every moment, a canvas unfolds,
A story of love that never grows old.
In the tapestry woven with threads of light,
We find our way through the darkest night.

A Symphony of Hearts

The rhythm of us, a tender song,
In perfect harmony, where we belong.
With every heartbeat, a pulse divine,
In this love renewed, your heart is mine.

The symphony swells, a sweet embrace,
As time slows down in this sacred space.
With every whisper, a promise made,
In the glow of love, all fears do fade.

CHAPTER TEN

Dare to Love Again

Whispers of Renewal

In twilight's glow, where shadows dance,
I find my heart in a second chance.
With whispered winds, I hear love's call,
A gentle promise to rise, not fall.

Taste the sweetness of morning light,
Feel the warmth of hope, a soft delight.
See the petals, fresh blooms in spring,
Hear the song of joy that love can bring.

Brave the Unknown

With courage clad in colors bright,

I step beyond the veil of night.

A heart once bruised now beats anew,

In the tender glow of love's debut.

Taste the thrill of uncharted paths,

Feel the pulse of a heart that laughs.

See the stars ignite the skies,

Hear the softest sighs as love replies.

Resilient Heartbeat

A heartbeat echoes, steady, strong,

In rhythm with a love-sown song.

Through trials faced and tears I've shed,

I rise anew, where angels tread.

Taste the freedom, bittersweet,

Feel the magic in each heartbeat.

See the dawn break, colors bloom,

Hear the whispers that chase the gloom.

Embrace the Light

With open arms, I greet the dawn,
In every moment, a chance reborn.
The past is but a fleeting shade,
In love's embrace, my fears will fade.

Taste the laughter on lips so near,
Feel the comfort, the warmth sincere.
See the promise in every gaze,
Hear the symphony of love's sweet praise.

Dare to Love Again

So here I stand, a heart laid bare,
With every breath, I choose to dare.
To love again, to risk the fall,
For in this journey, I'll have it all.

Taste the joy in every tear,
Feel the power of love held dear.
See the beauty in each embrace,
Hear the echo of a love-filled space.

Final Note

Dear Reader,

Thank you for sharing this journey,
for lingering in these lines of hope and healing.
If these words stirred your heart or lifted your spirit,
I'd be grateful if you shared your thoughts with
others.

Every review is a gift, a ripple of connection,
and it helps this book find its way to new hearts.

With gratitude and warmth,
Taylor Quill

About the Author

Taylor Quill is a contemporary poet and writer known for her evocative and heartfelt explorations of love, resilience, and personal growth. Born and raised in the Pacific Northwest, Taylor draws inspiration from the natural world and the complexities of human experience.

With a background in creative writing and psychology, Taylor's work is infused with empathy, vulnerability, and a deep understanding of the human condition. Her poetry invites readers to reflect on their own journeys, embracing the beauty and complexity of life.

Dare to Love Again, Taylor's debut poetry collection, is a testament to her own experiences with heartbreak, healing, and the transformative power of love. When not writing, Taylor enjoys hiking, journaling, and sipping coffee in quiet cafes.